BECAUSE
HE LOVED YOU
FIRST

Victoria Hudson

ISBN 979-8-88832-343-4 (paperback)
ISBN 979-8-88832-344-1 (digital)

Copyright © 2023 by Victoria Hudson

All rights reserved. No part of this publication may be reproduced, distributed, or transmitted in any form or by any means, including photocopying, recording, or other electronic or mechanical methods without the prior written permission of the publisher. For permission requests, solicit the publisher via the address below.

Christian Faith Publishing
832 Park Avenue
Meadville, PA 16335
www.christianfaithpublishing.com

Printed in the United States of America

Introduction

As a person who wants to know God and as a believer in God, his Word is all we need to stand on.

God's Word is alive. God's Word is the very essence of who he is, and it's captured in the Bible. The Scripture states that it will accomplish everything he sent it to do. His Word has shown me through time for centuries that it's true. The Bible is a direct reflection of God's love for us. Have people debated it? Yes, they have, but it has not changed for centuries, and as you come to know him or his Word, you will find that he loves you no matter what.

As you read further, you will find or be reminded that, at the base of everything, God loves you. He created the heavens and the earth for his children, which are you and me. The Scripture (his Word) teaches that he knows everything about you: he knows the decisions, the choices, and the mistakes we make. It teaches us that he knew our end and our outcome, and because of that, he created the Bible and allowed his Son, Jesus Christ, to be born so that we would come to know him and his love for us. There are so many scriptures, prayers, and examples in the Bible of God's words for you that show that he knows and cares for you.

The below scriptures were chosen as examples of God's power, of God's love, and that he has a plan for you. Just seek him and learn his Word, which is a direct reflection of the purpose and plan he has for your life.

> I knew you before you were in your mother's womb, I know the number of hairs on your head, he gave us dominion over all things. (Jeremiah 1:5)

Affirmation: No matter who I am, no matter what I have done, no matter what my secret struggles are, God cares for me, God knows me, and God loves me.

Because He Loved You First

Not believing in God doesn't change anything.
Believing in God changes everything.

Try me and see that I will open up a window of blessings
you will not have room enough to contain.

Contents

Introduction	iii
You Were Chosen	1
The Word	2
God	7
Grace, Mercy, and Favor	10
Love	15
Prayer	19
Promises	23
Forgiveness	26
Faith and Trust	30
Encouragement and Strength	34
Healing	38
Prayer of Protection	43
Prayer of Repentance	45
Salvation	47
Glossary	49

You Were Chosen

But you are a chosen people, a royal priesthood, a holy nation, God's special possession, that you may declare the praises of him who called you out of darkness into his wonderful light. (1 Peter 2:9 NIV)

For you *are* a holy people to the LORD your God, and the LORD has chosen you to be a people for Himself, a special treasure above all the peoples who *are* on the face of the earth. (Deuteronomy 14:2 NKJV)

And we know that in all things God works for the good of those who love him, who have been called according to his purpose. For those God foreknew he also predestined to be conformed to the image of his Son, that he might be the firstborn among many brothers and sisters. And those he predestined, he also called; those he called, he also justified; those he justified, he also glorified. (Romans 8:28–30 NIV)

For I know the plans I have for you…plans for good and not for disaster, to give you hope and a future. (Jeremiah 29:11)

The Word

We must understand that God's Word is truly all we need. It encompasses every area of life. The Holy Bible teaches us that God's Word is him, that it is alive, and that it will accomplish everything he intended it to complete. Consider this: Words are our most common way to communicate. We read them, we speak and write words, and we even have sign language to express ourselves with words. Our very foundation was created by the spoken word of God. He spoke, and everything was created.

He is his Word, and in that, we will find everything. God's Word is our protection. Think of what you consider your greatest strength or weapon, and look at it this way: at what point have any of them saved you from a traumatic event in your life? He is our provider. The Word states that we will never have to lack or want any beneficial thing. Let me put it like this: Think of a time when you were looking back over your life or had a memory and wondered how you made it through. Did a relative suddenly send unexpected cash? Perhaps you met a stranger, and they met a need without even knowing it was a need. There were so many instances in your life when God was there, and you may not have realized it was him. When God says he is your provider, he is just that, but remember that he is the provider of all things big and small—friends and family. Only you know that moment and space in your life, that a way was made, and you were simply grateful—that's God. He is a part of every area of your life.

God's Word is our weapon—not our loved ones, not ourselves, nor is it education or even our wealth that protects us, but is in fact the Word of God. When you were facing divorce, did your education save your marriage? Maybe you are wealthy and have a terminally ill loved one, but all you could do was pray for them. How often have you relied on your parents or spouse and found that they did not always have the answers and were not always there to defend you? What I am saying is no matter what you have or accomplished, or regardless of whom you've put your trust in, at some point, it has failed us. All we must do is call on God's name. While our strengths or weapons of choice are from God, they can't protect us the way God does.

Affirmation: God help me believe in your Word. God help me trust in your word. God allow me to know you by your Word.

The Word—Special revelation from God, communication, an understood meaning

In the beginning was the Word, and the Word was with God, and the Word was God. He was with God in the beginning. Through him all things were made; without him nothing was made that has been made. In him was life, and that life was the light of all mankind. The light shines in the darkness, and the darkness has not overcome it. (John 1:1–5 NIV)

The Word became flesh and made his dwelling among us. We have seen his glory, the glory of the one and only Son, who came from the Father, full of grace and truth. (John 1:14 NIV)

For the word of God is alive and active. Sharper than any double-edged sword, it penetrates even to dividing soul and spirit, joints, and marrow; it judges the thoughts and attitudes of the heart. (Hebrews 4:12 NIV)

"For my thoughts are not your thoughts, neither are your ways my ways," declares the Lord. "As the heavens are higher than the earth, so are my ways higher than your ways and my thoughts than your thoughts." (Isaiah 55:8–9 NIV)

God will meet all your needs according to the riches of his glory in Christ Jesus. (Philippians 4:19 NIV)

God is our refuge and strength, an ever-present help in times of trouble. (Psalm 46:1 NIV)

So do not fear, for I am with you; do not be dismayed, for I am your God. I will strengthen you and help you; I will uphold you with my righteous right hand. (Isaiah 41:10 NIV)

My prayer:

God, in the name of Jesus, I thank you that your children may come to know you through your Word like never before. I thank you that as they meditate on the scriptures, your living Word may quicken their spirits and develop a hunger and a thirst for you. I thank you because they will come to know the love that you have for them, and in that, they will receive peace, knowledge, and understanding. As they read the Word, they will find the grace and mercy they desire every day—that it would answer some of the questions they may have about life and about you. Bless your child. Allow them to know that there is nothing they cannot bring before your throne.

Your prayer:

God

God is so many things to so many people, but he is also the same thing to all people. In short, not only is he the creator of all things, but he is our Father. When we talk or pray to God, we ask of things we would ask a loving father, who may be absent, maybe financially unable, or just incapable of providing for a multitude of reasons. However, everything your natural dad cannot provide, your heavenly Father God can. Ask yourself, have you ever prayed for things like a car or a house? Perhaps you prayed about depression or hurt. Maybe you prayed for wisdom or direction for something specific. When you got it, your words were: "Thank you, God," or "Thank you, Father God." We seek God in all areas of our lives, even when we do not realize it. Below are different names of God that have been used biblically to describe God as not only a provider but also our Father. God is everything and everything we need.

Affirmation: God, you are the Father of all fathers. I will trust in you and your Word as I seek to understand you more through your Word.

God—Piety, the being perfect in power, wisdom, and goodness

Jehovah:

"I am who I am"… "The Lord, the God of your fathers—the God of Abraham, the God of Isaac, and the God of Jacob—has sent me to you." "This is my name forever, the name you shall call me from generation to generation." (Exodus 3:14–15 NIV)

Omnipotent, Omniscience, Omnipresence (all power, all present, all-knowing God).

Alpha and Omega, the beginning, and the ending, saith the Lord, which is, and which was, and which is to come, the Almighty. (Revelations 1:8)

Jehovah Adonai—My Lord the Sovereign (Genesis 15)
Jehovah Rapha—The Lord My Healer (Exodus 15)
Jehovah Jireh—My Provider (Genesis 22)
Jehovah Nissi—My Victory, My Banner (Exodus 17)
Jehovah Tsidkenu—My Righteousness (Jeremiah 23)
Jehovah M'Kaddesh—My Sanctifier (Exodus 31)
El-Elyon—The Most High God, the possessor of the heavens and the earth, the everlasting God, the living God, the merciful God, the faithful God. You are truth, justice, righteousness, and perfection. The Highest sovereign of the heavens and earth.

But when he, the Spirit of truth, comes, he will guide you into all the truth. (John 16:13 NIV)

My prayer:

Father, I pray that your children will come to know who you are and that they will know and understand your perfect love for them. I pray that they will understand the kindness that shines through you and your Word. You are all-powerful and all-knowing; nothing is impossible for you, Lord. Reveal to your children who you are in a new way. Let them see you, Lord, with new eyes so that they may know that you are God and that you can supply all their needs according to your riches and glory in Christ Jesus.

Your prayer:

Grace, Mercy, and Favor

The words *grace, mercy,* and *favor* are such very common terms when we speak of God blessing us, but have you thought about or reminded yourself that when you remove the hunger or need for material things, these very words are a direct description of how he feels about you? No matter the problem, no matter the situation, no matter the hurt, shame, or guilt you carry, he cares for you. He understands what you are going through and will help you. These words allow you to go to the Father about anything. They encompass the love God has for us. They are the words we should live by with one another. These words cover everything we need from God. They carry us through every area of our lives—God's grace, mercy, and favor in our lives. Review the below scriptures as I pray that God reveals the power of his love for you.

Affirmation: God loves me and has compassion for me. God will forgive me, and he will bless me with kindness.

Grace, Mercy, and Favor—God's free and unmerited favor, compassionate, forgiving, kindness, approval, partiality, showing special, or friendly regard

Grace

For it is by grace you have been saved, through faith—and this is not from yourselves, it is the gift of God—not by works, so that no one can boast. (Ephesians 2: 8–9)

The love and mercy are given to us by God because God desires us to have them, not necessarily because of anything we have done to earn it. It is not a created substance of any kind. It is an attribute of God that is most manifest in the salvation of sinners.

But to each one of us grace has been given as Christ apportioned it. (Ephesians 4:7)

For the grace of God has appeared that offers salvation to all people. (Titus 2:11)

And after you have suffered a little while, the God of all grace, who has called you to his eternal glory in Christ, will himself restore, confirm, strengthen, and establish you. (1 Peter 5:10)

And from his fullness we have all received, grace upon grace. (John 1:16)

We believe it is through the grace of our Lord Jesus that we are saved, just as they are. (Acts 15:11)

Mercy and Favor

> The Lord, the Lord God, merciful and gracious, long suffering, and abounding in goodness and truth, keeping mercy for thousands, forgiving iniquity and transgression and sin. (Exodus 34:6–7)

> But God, being rich in mercy, because of the great love with which he loved us, even when we were dead in our trespasses, made us alive together with Christ—by grace you have been saved Ephesians 2:4-5

> The Lord passed before him and proclaimed, "The Lord, the Lord, a God merciful and gracious, slow to anger, and abounding in steadfast love and faithfulness." (Exodus 34:6)

> Let not mercy and truth forsake you; bind them around your neck, write them on the tablet of your heart, and so find favor and high esteem in the sight of God and man. (Proverbs 3:3–4)

> Blessed be the God and Father of our Lord Jesus Christ, the Father of mercies and God of all comfort, who comforts us in all our tribulation, that we may be able to comfort those who are in any trouble, with the comfort with which we ourselves are comforted by God. (2 Corinthians 1:3–4)

> The Lord is gracious and full of compassion, slow to anger and great in mercy. The Lord is good to all, and His tender mercies are over all His works. (Psalm 145:8–9)

Through the Lord's mercies we are not consumed, because His compassions fail not. They are new every morning; great is Your faithfulness. (Lamentations 3:22–23)

Who is a God like You, pardoning iniquity and passing over the transgression of the remnant of His heritage? He does not retain His anger forever, because He delights in mercy. He will again have compassion on us and will subdue our iniquities. You will cast all our sins into the depths of the sea. (Micah 7:18–19)

My prayer:

God, I thank you for the grace, mercy, and favor you've shown to us all. Thank you for forgiving us when we did not forgive ourselves or one another. Thank you for all that you have done. God, we thank you for the kindness that you have shown us in our everyday lives. Father, I thank you that as you reveal to us your loving kindness shown through your grace, your mercy, and your favor, we will start to receive them and fully understand them so that we'll be able to experience your love in a new way. I thank you that as you protect us, guide us, and bless us, we will humble ourselves before you and learn to share that same loving kindness with individuals who cross our path or are in our lives. Lord, thank you for a love we all so strongly desire. Bless the individual reading this prayer in Jesus's name, amen.

Your prayer:

_____
_____
_____
_____
_____
_____
_____
_____
_____
_____
_____
_____
_____
_____
_____
_____
_____
_____
_____

Love

God's love for us is so complete that it's hard to comprehend and even harder to explain, but as we start to realize that love, it changes us forever. It does not make us perfect, but it changes so many things about ourselves, the way we view others, and most importantly, the relationship we have with God. I am confident that God loves each and every one of us no matter who we are, no matter what we have done, and no matter what we have been through; his love is complete. His love is perfect.

Many of us do not understand how God feels about us because we do not know his Word, because we don't know him. Some know his Word but feel unworthy of his love because of guilt and shame. It could be because of traditional teachings that focus on hell and damnation, among other things. Whatever your reason for not receiving God's true love for you, it does not change the fact that he truly loves you. There are countless scriptures and examples of his love through his Word. There are too many to choose from, but he wrote a book expressing his great love for you and me: the Bible.

Affirmation: No matter who I am, no matter what I have done, no matter what my secret struggles are, God cares for me, knows me, and loves me.

Love—Devotion, strong affection

> For God so loved the world that he gave his one and only Son, that whoever believes in him shall not perish but have eternal life. For God did not send his Son into the world to condemn the world, but to save the world through him. (John 3:16–17)
>
> God demonstrates his own love for us in this: While we were still sinners, Christ died for us. (Romans 5:8)
>
> Give thanks to the Lord, for He is good: His love endures forever. (Psalm 107:1)
>
> For great is his love toward us, and the faithfulness of the Lord endures forever. (Psalm 117:2)
>
> Humble yourselves, therefore, under God's mighty hand, that he may lift you up in due time. Cast all your anxiety on him because he cares for you. (1 Peter 5:6–7)
>
> But there is a friend who sticks closer than a brother. (Proverbs 18:24)
>
> "Though the mountains be shaken, and the hills be removed, yet my unfailing love for you will not be shaken nor my covenant of peace be removed," says the Lord, who has compassion on you. (Isaiah 54:10)
>
> But because of his great love for us, God, who is rich in mercy, made us alive with Christ even

when we were dead in transgressions—it is by grace you have been saved. (Ephesians 2:4–5)

In all these things we are more than conquerors through him who loved us. For I am convinced that neither death nor life, neither angels nor demons, neither the present nor the future, nor any powers, neither height nor depth, nor anything else in all creation, will be able to separate us from the love of God that is in Christ Jesus our Lord. (Romans 8:37–39)

My prayer:

> I pray that out of his glorious riches he may strengthen you with power through his Spirit in your inner being so that Christ may dwell in your hearts through faith. And I pray that you, being rooted and established in love may have power, together with all the Lord's holy people to grasp how wide and long and high and deep is the love of Christ, and to know this love that surpasses knowledge—that you may be filled to the measure of all the fullness of God. (Ephesians 3:16–19)

Your prayer:

Prayer

The most common and most effective way to communicate with God is through prayer. There are many conversations or traditions on how we should pray, but quite simply, prayer is a conversation with God; Prayer is absolute. The Word teaches how to pray, what to pray for, and to bring everything in our hearts and mind to Christ. Prayer is so important that Jesus left instructions and actual prayers we could pray when we are calling out to *God*. Prayer helps us build trust in our relationship with God. It helps us get through difficult times in our lives. Prayer gives us peace. Prayer gives us answers. And most importantly, prayer allows us to speak with the Father. Conversation with God is so important that he gave us a direct line to his ear. While we can seek out others for prayer, we no longer must rely solely on authority figures such as priests or pastors, nor do we have to complete biblical rituals from the Old Testament to be considered righteous before going to the throne. Prayer not only allows us to speak to God, but it allows us to hear from God. Remember that prayer is a conversation, and normally, conversation means to speak and listen to one another. I do not know where I would be if I didn't have prayer. For me, it is as necessary as breathing. Learn to talk to God about everything.

Affirmation: I will bring everything to God in prayer. I will find my peace and joy in prayer. I will listen to God's words in prayer.

Prayer—Communicating with God

> In the same way, the Spirit helps us in our weakness. We do not know what we ought to pray for, but the Spirit himself intercedes for us through wordless groans. And he who searches our hearts knows the mind of the Spirit, because the Spirit intercedes for God's people in accordance with the will of God. (Romans 8:26–27)

> Then you will call on me and come and pray to me, and I will listen to you. (Jeremiah 29:12)

> I call on you, My God, for you will answer me; turn your ear to me and hear my prayer. (Psalm 17:6)

> He will respond to the prayer of the destitute; He will not despise their plea. (Psalm 102:17)

> Rejoice always, pray continually, give thanks in all circumstances; for this is God's will for you in Christ Jesus. (1 Thessalonians 5:17–18)

> Pray in the Spirit at all times, with every kind of prayer and petition. To this end, stay alert with all perseverance in your prayers for all the saints. (Ephesians 6:18)

> Rejoice in the Lord always. I will say it again: Rejoice! Let your gentleness be evident to all. The Lord is near. Do not be anxious about anything, but in every situation, by prayer and petition, with thanksgiving, present your requests to God. And the peace of God, which transcends all understanding, will guard your hearts and your minds in Christ Jesus. (Philippians 4:4–7)

When you pray, go into your room, close the door, and pray to your Father, who is unseen… "This, then, is how you should pray: Our Father in heaven, hallowed be your name, your kingdom come, your will be done, on earth as it is in heaven Give us today our daily bread. And forgive us our debts, as we also have forgiven our debtors and lead us not into temptation but deliver us from the evil one." (Matthew 6:6, 9–13)

The Lord is my shepherd, I lack nothing. He makes me lie down in green pastures, he leads me beside quiet waters, he refreshes my soul. He guides me along the right paths for his name's sake. Even though I walk through the darkest valley, I will fear no evil, for you are with me; your rod and your staff, they comfort me. You prepare a table before me in the presence of my enemies. You anoint my head with oil, my cup overflows. Surely your goodness and love will follow me all the days of my life, and I will dwell in the house of the Lord forever. (Psalm 23)

Read Psalm 25.

My prayer:

Father, I thank you for the ability to come before your throne directly. I thank you that my friend will understand that being in your presence comes about with prayer. I thank you because they will understand that at your feet is the most high place. I thank you, Lord, that you have given them the gift of prayer, which is simply talking to you—that in prayer, there is peace, there is deliverance, there is joy, and there is victory. I thank you, Father, because they will find the words to pour their hearts out to you in prayer. Lord, I thank you that we are all able to always come to you in prayer, no matter the situation. Bless them, their hearts, and their prayers, Lord. In Jesus's name. Amen.

Your prayer:

Promises

God's promises to us are true and real, just like his Word is living, so are his promises. I have found that the very promises of God have protected us. They have healed and delivered us. They have given us joy and salvation. The promises of God have gotten us through some of the most difficult seasons of our lives. As you learn his Word, you will see that protection, peace, blessing, and victory—the preceding list—are but a few of the promises from the heavenly Father. One of my most meditated scriptures from the Bible is Matthew chapter 6. These verses reflect a promise from God on how well he will take care of us. It goes on to explain that if he cares for the birds of the air and the flowers that are clothed, how much more will he take care of us? It also advises us to have faith in him and not to worry because he will care for us. I love that promise because it reminds me that God will take care of everything—that every detail and need about me matters to him and that he will make a way. We just must trust in him and his promises. Our prayer request to God is just that, a request, but his promises are guaranteed, and all we must do is believe that and stand on it. He never fails us.

Affirmation: I believe in God's promises. Lord, help me to know and receive your promises. I will trust in God's promises.

Promises—To pledge or give, assurance, covenant

> The Holy Spirit also testifies to us about this. First, he says: "This is the covenant I will make with them after that time, says the Lord. I will put my laws in their hearts, and I will write them on their minds." Then he adds: "Their sins and lawless acts I will remember no more. And where these have been forgiven, sacrifice for sin is no longer necessary." (Hebrews 10:15–18)

> For no matter how many promises God has made, they are "Yes" in Christ. And so, through him the "Amen" is spoken by us to the glory of God. Now it is God who makes both us and you stand firm in Christ. He anointed us, set his seal of ownership on us, and put his Spirit in our hearts as a deposit guaranteeing what is to come. (2 Corinthians 1:20–22)

> So do not fear, for I am with you; do not be dismayed, for I am your God. I will strengthen you and help you; I will uphold you with my righteous right hand. (Isaiah 41:10)

> But now, this is what the Lord says—he who created you, Jacob, he who formed you, Israel: "Do not fear, for I have redeemed you; I have summoned you by name; you are mine. When you pass through the waters, I will be with you; and when you pass through the rivers, they will not sweep over you. When you walk through the fire, you will not be burned; the flames will not set you ablaze." (Isaiah 43:1–2)

My prayer:

Lord, I pray that my friends would come to understand and walk in the promises you have for them. That they will see and know through your promises that you have loved them since the beginning of time. I pray that they know from your Word that you will see them through it all—that you have made a way to protect and strengthen them. Lord, I thank you because they will see that they have nothing to fear because you are their Father and that you will keep them. Thank you, Lord, that you would remind them that there is no sin too great for you and that no temptation will overcome them. Always remind them that you are the victory they need to overcome all things. I pray that they know that in their hearts that you have a plan for them. In Jesus's name, I pray.

Your prayer:

Forgiveness

God's forgiveness is unlimited, and I thank him for it every day. His forgiveness is nothing like that of human beings. It is continual, and it's complete. The first thing I want you to know is there is no sin you or I could commit that would not allow God to forgive us. While we may find forgiveness difficult with certain acts or certain things, God promises to forgive us and does forgive us once we accept him into our lives. With his forgiveness, comes forgetfulness. His Word promises that God will forgive all our iniquity and remember our sins no more (Jeremiah 31). In Micah 7, it states that God would cast our sins into the deepest sea. Imagine that God loves us so much that he forgives us when we do not forgive ourselves and don't forgive others. No matter what you have done, God has room to forgive us of our wrongs and make them right. Please take a moment to apologize (repent) to the Father for anything you carry in your heart toward yourself or others. He loves you and wants you to rid yourself of any burden or guilt you find hard to forgive, or if you find it hard to receive forgiveness. His forgiveness is like no others and is unlimited.

Affirmation: I will receive the gift of God's forgiveness. God will teach me to forgive others and help me to walk in forgiveness for myself and others.

Forgiveness—To pardon or acquittal of sins

> But because of his great love for us, God, who is rich in mercy, made us alive with Christ even when we were dead in transgressions—it is by grace you have been saved. And God raised us up with Christ and seated us with him in the heavenly realms in Christ Jesus, in order that in the coming ages he might show the incomparable riches of his grace, expressed in his kindness to us in Christ Jesus. For it is by grace you have been saved, through faith—and this is not from yourselves, it is the gift of God—not by works, so that no one can boast. For we are God's handiwork, created in Christ Jesus to do good works, which God prepared in advance for us to do. (Ephesians 2:4–10)

> The LORD works righteousness and justice for all the oppressed… The LORD is compassionate and gracious, slow to anger, abounding in love. He will not always accuse, nor will he harbor his anger forever; he does not treat us as our sins deserve or repay us according to our iniquities. (Psalm 103:6, 8–10)

> If we claim to be without sin, we deceive ourselves and the truth is not in us. If we confess our sins, he is faithful and just and will forgive us our sins and purify us from all unrighteousness. (1 John 1:8–9)

> The Holy Spirit also testifies to us about this. First, he says: "This is the covenant I will make with them after that time, says the Lord. I will put my laws in their hearts, and I will write

them on their minds." Then he adds: "Their sins and lawless acts I will remember no more." And where these have been forgiven, sacrifice for sin is no longer necessary. (Hebrews 10:15)

Who is a God like you, who pardons sin and forgives the transgression of the remnant of his inheritance? You do not stay angry forever but delight to show mercy. You will again have compassion on us; you will tread our sins underfoot and hurl all our iniquities into the depths of the sea. (Micah 7:18–19)

Read Psalm 51.

My prayer:

Heavenly Father, I thank you for your grace and mercy that is renewed daily. I thank you, Father, because they will come to understand that there is no condemnation for those you love. Father, allow them to repent and forgive themselves the way that you have forgiven them. Show them, Lord, that you care for them and love them. Let them not be ashamed or afraid because they have been made worthy by your great love. Open their hearts so that they may receive all that you have for them in Jesus's name, I pray. Amen.

Your prayer:

Faith and Trust

Having trust and faith in God is not the same as trusting a loved one such as a parent, a spouse, a sibling, or a best friend. Having faith in God means receiving all that he has for you. It means receiving the love he has for you and all that comes along with it. Trusting in God means no matter what happens, no matter what you go through, you know that he is there for you, carrying you through it, and he will give you a greater victory when it's time. Trusting God and having faith in God means while a specific prayer was not answered the way you wanted, it was answered for the greater good of all concerned.

Isaiah 55:8–9 states,

> "For my thoughts are not your thoughts, neither are your ways my ways," declares the Lord. "As the heavens are higher than the earth, so are my ways higher than your ways and my thoughts than your thoughts."

Our faith and trust in God mean believing in him at all times—good and bad, knowing that he has our back, that he knows everything about us, and all will work together for our good in the end. Faith and trust are paramount to our relationship with Christ and others.

Affirmation: I will trust in God. I will have faith in God's Word. I will receive God's forgiveness and promises. I will believe in his Word.

Faith and Trust—Reliance, loyalty, to have complete trust in God, to have confidence in, to have hope in, to believe

Now faith is the substance of things hoped for, the evidence of things not seen. Through faith we understand that the worlds were framed by the word of God, so that things which are seen were not made of things which do appear. (Hebrews 11:1–3)

Looking unto Jesus the author and finisher of our faith, who for the joy that was set before him endured the cross, despising the shame, and is set down at the right hand of the throne of God. (Hebrews 12:2)

Truly I tell you, if you have faith and do not doubt, not only can you do what was done to the fig tree, but also you can say to this mountain, "Go, throw yourself into the sea," and it will be done. If you believe, you will receive whatever you ask for in prayer. (Matthew 21:21–22)

Consequently, faith comes from hearing the message, and the message is heard through the word about Christ. (Romans 10:17)

If any of you lacks wisdom, you should ask God, who gives generously to all without finding fault, and it will be given to you. But when you ask, you must believe and not doubt, because the one who doubts is like a wave of the sea, blown and tossed by the wind. (James 1:5–6)

Trust in the Lord with all your heart and lean not on your own understanding; in all your ways acknowledge him and he will make your path straight. (Proverbs 3:5–6)

I am your strength and your shield; let your heart trust in me, and I will help you. Let your heart leap for joy, and with song give me praise. (Psalm 28:7)

My grace is sufficient for you, for my power is made perfect in weakness. (2 Corinthians 12:9)

But blessed is the one who trusts in the Lord, whose confidence is in him. (Jeremiah 17:7)

The Lord is good, a refuge in times of trouble. He cares for those who trust in him. (Nahum 1:7)

Let us draw near to God with a sincere heart and with the full assurance that faith brings, having our hearts sprinkled to cleanse us from a guilty conscience and having our bodies washed with pure water. Let us hold unswervingly to the hope we profess, for he who promised is faithful. (Hebrews 10:22–23)

My prayer:

    Father, I thank you that trust and faith go hand in hand. Teach us, Lord, to trust in you and have faith in you with our whole hearts. I pray that as my friend starts to trust in you, they will find there is joy and peace in knowing you. I thank you, Lord, that as they grow in who you are, they will find the battle is not theirs but yours, Lord. They will know through you that there is victory in every situation they come across. Teach us, Lord, to know you, to trust, and to build our faith in you. For these things, I pray in Jesus's name.

Your prayer:

Encouragement and Strength

In life, we will all have challenges and will find our backs against the wall. Sometimes, there's no easy fix or quick answer. And because of our nature, we often find ourselves seeking solace in people or things that doesn't help you or the situation. It may seem like it does at that moment, but when you look back on the times you sought counsel from a loved one or leader in your life, it didn't always help or wasn't the right answer. Some of us have confided in a friend and found that you felt worse or the situation was magnified. Then some of us turn to drugs and alcohol to ease the anguish, stress, or hurt we are going through, which we all know, in the end made it much worse.

Affirmation: God is my strength. I will stand on God's Word as my encouragement. The joy of the Lord is my strength.

Encouragement and Strength—To strengthen or stimulate

Do you not know? Have you not heard? The LORD is the everlasting God, the Creator of the ends of the earth. He will not grow tired or weary, and his understanding no one can fathom. He gives strength to the weary and increases the power of the weak. Even youths grow tired and weary, and young men stumble and fall; but those who hope in the LORD will renew their strength. They will soar on wings like eagles; they will run and not grow weary; they will walk and not be faint. (Isaiah 40:28–32)

I can do all things through Christ who strengthens me. (Philippians 4:13)

Peace, I leave with you; my peace I give you. I do not give to you as the world gives. Do not let your hearts be troubled and do not be afraid. (John 14:27)

Be joyful in hope, patient in affliction, faithful in prayer. (Romans 12:12)

I have told you these things, so that in me you may have peace. In this world you will have trouble. But take heart! I have overcome the world. (John 16:33)

Be strong and courageous! Do not be afraid or discouraged. For I, the Lord your God, your Father will be with you wherever you go. (Joshua 1:9)

Do not let your hearts be troubled. You believe in God; believe also in me. My Father's house has many rooms; if that were not so, would I have told you that I am going there to prepare a place for you? And if I go and prepare a place for you, I will come back and take you to be with me that you also may be where I am. You know the way to the place where I am going. (John 14:1–4)

Let us therefore come boldly unto the throne pf grace, that we may obtain mercy, and find grace to help in a time of need. (Hebrews 4:16)

For I have not given you a spirit of fear and timidity, but of power, love, and self-discipline. (2 Timothy 1:7)

The name of the Lord is a strong tower; the righteous man runs into it and is safe. (Proverbs 18:10)

My grace is sufficient for you, for my power is made perfect in weakness. Therefore, I will boast all the more gladly about my weaknesses, so that Christ's power may rest on me. (2 Corinthians 12:9)

Lift your eyes to the hills, where your help comes from. Your help comes from me the Lord, the Maker of heaven and earth. I will not let your foot slip, I watch over you will not slumber, neither will I sleep. The Lord watches over you, I am the shade at your right hand, the sun will not harm you by day nor the moon by night. Child I will keep you from all harm, I will watch over your life; you're coming and going both now and forever more. (Psalm 121:1–8)

My grace is sufficient for you, for my power is made perfect in weakness. Therefore, I will boast all the more gladly about my weaknesses, so that Christ's power may rest on me. (2 Corinthians 12:9)

My prayer:

God, I thank you that the joy of the Lord is our strength. I thank you, Father, in times of trial and tribulation; with heartbreak and sorrow, we can count on you to get us through. Lord, thank you that in you, we can find rest and peace. Father, thank you for your word that strengthens and guides us in all things. Lord, I thank you because my friend will know that all things are possible through Jesus Christ, who strengthens us, and that when they find themselves in need, they will turn to your dear Son—a friend, closer than a brother, and someone who cares and knows what they're going through. Strengthen and encourage them. Remind them that you are there in the good times and the bad times. In Jesus's name, I pray. Amen.

Your prayer:

_____
_____
_____
_____
_____
_____
_____
_____
_____
_____
_____
_____
_____
_____
_____
_____
_____
_____
_____

Healing

I have given a lot of thought on how to discuss healing and have come up short because the healing of Jesus Christ covers every faucet of our lives. Jesus has healed and offers healing for us all in every way imaginable. His gift of healing allows us to be healed from all diseases: physical, emotional, mental, and spiritual. In my research on healing, I've found that while it is more pronounced in the New Testament, it's found in the Old Testament as well, which supports the idea that God has been our healer and deliverer since the beginning of time.

One of my many finds is that Jesus healed the believer and the nonbeliever time and time again. He was able to heal sick people when they had run out of options, and he was their only hope. He healed people for whom others had given up hope for. He delivered people who struggled with incurable diseases, mental disorders, and strongholds (in modern terms, it means addictions, mental issues, brokenheartedness, etc.). Yes, he even delivered people who were under spiritual attack. Another finding for me in reading the scriptures of Jesus's ministry and healing was that each person he healed had faith in him, whether they walked in faith for themselves or a loved one. Scripture shows in multiple scriptures that Jesus advised them that their faith made them whole or that their faith healed their loved ones and to go in peace.

I must say that in my lifetime, I have experienced and witnessed Jesus's healing for myself, those that I have loved, and those that I have prayed for that others loved. If you or someone you know needs healing in their lives for anything, pray to God on their behalf and allow his will to be done. The most compelling or convincing fact for me was when I learned about the persecution of Jesus Christ on the cross. Everything that he endured, from the beating to being nailed to the cross, reflects healing power for every area of our lives. What I can promise is that when you really learn what the thirty-three stripes on his back provided, the nails in his hands offered, or even the crown of thorns did, it will change your heart.

Affirmation: I believe Jesus is my healer.

Healing—To mend, to cure, to make whole, return to original state.

> He was pierced for our transgressions, he was crushed for our iniquities; the punishment that brought us peace was on him, and by his wounds we are healed. (Isaiah 53:5)

> So, if the Son sets you free, you are free indeed. (John 8:36)

> The Spirit of the Sovereign Lord is on me, because the Lord has anointed me to proclaim good news to the poor. (Luke 4:18)

> He has sent me to bind up the brokenhearted, to proclaim freedom for the captives and release from darkness for the prisoners. (Isaiah 61:1)

> Go back and report to John what you hear and see: The blind receive sight, the lame walk, those who have leprosy are cleansed, the deaf hear, the dead are raised, and the good news is proclaimed to the poor. Blessed is anyone who does not stumble on account of me. (Matthew 11:4–6)

> I pray that you may enjoy good health and that all may go well with you, even as your soul is getting along well. (3 John 1:2)

> Worship the Lord your God, and his blessing will be on your food and water. I will take away sickness from among you, and none will miscarry or be barren in your land. (Exodus 23:25–26)

Spiritual or Mental Healing

Spiritual Healing

- Heal me for my bones are in agony (Psalm 6:2).
- He heals the broken hearted (Psalm 147:3).
- The tongue of the wise brings healing. (Proverbs 12:18).
- Seen his ways, but I will heal him (Isaiah 57:18).
- By his wounds you have been healed (1 Peter 2:24).
- Evil spirits and all of them were healed (Acts 5:16).

Physical Healing

- And seen your tears I will heal you (2 Kings 20:5).
- And heal all your diseases (Psalm 103:3).
- He sent forth his word and healed them (Psalm 107:20).
- Jesus heals physical and spiritual sickness (Matthew 9:2; Luke 8:43–48).
- Jesus heals broken lives (Matthew 15:29–31).
- Importance of spiritual health (Matthew 15:16–20).
- For I am the Lord who heals you (Exodus 15:26).

Faith Healing

- Said to him Jesus Christ has healed you (Acts 9:34).
- Evil spirits and all of them were healed (Acts 5:16).
- Many are the afflictions of the righteous, But the Lord delivers him out of them all (Psalm 34:19).
- Said to him Jesus Christ has healed you (Acts 9:34).
- Evil spirits and all of them were healed (Acts 5:16).

My prayer:

Father, I thank you for healing us. I thank you for what your dear Son, Jesus, did on the cross that we may be healed, saved, set free, and delivered from anything and everything that is not of you, Lord. I thank you, Lord, that you would heal the person reading this prayer right now and will heal any of their loved ones from anything they may be struggling with that hinders or prevents them from living the life you called them to live. Open our eyes, Lord, that we can see and receive every good and perfect gift that comes from your healing. I thank you, Lord, that as we study these scriptures, our eyes will be opened, and we will be enlightened to your love and miraculous touch of healing and deliverance. In Jesus's name, I pray. Amen.

Your prayer:

_____
_____
_____
_____
_____
_____
_____
_____
_____
_____
_____
_____
_____
_____
_____
_____
_____
_____
_____
_____

Prayer of Protection

Armour of God

Finally, be strong in the Lord and in his mighty power. Put on the full armor of God, so that you can take your stand against the devil's schemes. For our struggle is not against flesh and blood, but against the rulers, against the authorities, against the powers of this dark world and against the spiritual forces of evil in the heavenly realms. Therefore, put on the full armor of God, so that when the day of evil comes, you may be able to stand your ground, and after you have done everything, to stand. Stand firm then, with the belt of truth buckled around your waist, with the breastplate of righteousness in place, and with your feet fitted with the readiness that comes from the gospel of peace. In addition to all this, take up the shield of faith, with which you can extinguish all the flaming arrows of the evil one. Take the helmet of salvation and the sword of the Spirit, which is the word of God. And pray in the Spirit on all occasions with all kinds of prayers and requests. Be alert and always keep on praying for all the Lord's people. (Ephesians 6:10–18)

Prayer of Protection

Those who live in the shelter of the Most High will find rest in the shadow of the Almighty. This I declare about the Lord: He alone is my refuge, my place of safety; he is my God, and I trust him. For he will rescue you from every trap and protect you from deadly disease. He will cover you with his feathers. He will shelter you with his wings. His faithful promises are your armor and protection. Do not be afraid of the terrors of the night, nor the arrow that flies in the day. Do not dread the disease that stalks in darkness, nor the disaster that strikes at midday. Though a thousand fall at your side, though ten thousand are dying around you, these evils will not touch you. Just open your eyes and see how the wicked are punished. If you make the Lord your refuge, if you make the Most High your shelter, no evil will conquer you; no plague will come near your home. For he will order his angels to protect you wherever you go. They will hold you up with their hands, so you won't even hurt your foot on a stone. You will trample upon lions and cobras; you will crush fierce lions and serpents under your feet! The Lord says, "I will rescue those who love me, I will protect those who trust in my name. When they call on me, I will answer; I will be with them in trouble. I will rescue and honor them. I will reward them with a long life and give them my salvation. (Psalm 91)

Prayer of Repentance

Have mercy on me, O God according to your unfailing love; according to your great compassion blot out my transgressions. Wash away all my iniquity and cleanse me from my sin. For I know my transgressions, and my sin is always before me. Against you, you only, have I sinned and done what is evil in your sight; so you are right in your verdict and justified when you judge. Surely, I was sinful at birth, sinful from the time my mother conceived me. Yet you desired faithfulness even in the womb; you taught me wisdom that secret place. Cleanse me with hyssop, and I will be clean; wash me, and I will be whiter than snow. Let me hear joy and gladness; let the bones you have crushed rejoice. Hide your face from my sins and blot out all my iniquity. Create in me a pure heart, O God, and renew a steadfast spirit within me. Do not cast me from your presence or take your Holy Spirit from me. Restore to me the joy of your salvation and grant me a willing spirit, to sustain me. Then I will teach transgressors your ways, so that sinners will turn back to you. Deliver me from the guilt of bloodshed, O God, you who are God my Savior, and my tongue will sing of your righteousness. Open my lips, Lord, and my mouth will declare your praise. You do not delight in sacrifice, or I would bring it; you do not take pleasure in burnt offerings. My sacrifice, O God, is a broken spirit; a broken and contrite heart you, God, will not despise. May it please you to prosper Zion, to build up the walls of Jerusalem. Then you will delight in the sacrifices of the righteous. (Psalm 51)

Salvation

If you declare with your mouth, "Jesus is Lord," and believe in your heart that God raised him from the dead, you will be saved. For it is with your heart that you believe and are justified, and it is with your mouth that you profess your faith and are saved. As Scripture says, "Anyone who believes in him will never be put to shame." For there is no difference between Jew and Gentile—the same Lord is Lord of all and richly blesses all who call on him, for, "Everyone who calls on the name of the Lord will be saved." (Romans 10:9–13)

Glossary

chosen. To decide or select; to be selected for a sovereign purpose
deliverance. To rescue, to liberate or set free, to redeem
encouragement. To strengthen or stimulate
faith. Reliance, loyalty, to have complete trust in God
faithfulness. Devotion, loyal, worthy of trust
favor. Kindness, approval, partiality, showing special or friendly regard
forgiveness. To pardon or acquittal of sins
God. Piety, the being perfect in power, wisdom, and goodness
grace. Gods free and unmerited favor
healing. To mend, to cure, to make whole, return to original state
holy. Consecrated, set apart for scared use, sacred
love. Devotion, strong affection
mercy. Compassionate, forgiving
prayer. Communicating with God
promises. To pledge or give, assurance, covenant
protection. To shield from danger
salvation. Rescue, preserve, deliverance from danger or difficulty, freed from the penalty of sin
strength. Endurance, strong, the ability to withstand hardship or adversity, to carry on despite suffering
trust. To have confidence in, to have hope in, to believe in
unfailing. Dependable, unending, never ceasing
wisdom. Godly or good judgement, good use of knowledge, recognize right from wrong
Word of God. Special revelation from God, communication an understood meaning

Let me start by saying that I love the Lord, and the Lord loves me, and he loves you too. I am not by any measure without sin, and I do experience some of the same problems and emotions you go through. We all, at some point in our lives, share some of the same joys, hurts, disappointments, and emotions that life experiences may cause. Whoever you are and wherever you may be in life, God's love is unfailing for all, and that love is unfailing during your best seasons as well as your most troubled seasons.

We all have our way of sharing God's Word; we all have our opinions and points of view about who God is and what his Word means to us. We have a way of measuring ourselves based on teachings from different avenues in our lives. It could be from the church, Christian classes, family members, friends, books, movies, etc. Whatever measure you use, it does not change God's love for you.

Because He Loved You First is my way of sharing God with you. It is my way of reminding you of God's love in the most basic sense by using his Word. If you are in a season in your life where you feel that you do not know God, you may want to know more about God, or even that he doesn't hear you, these are scriptures that are often meditated on or used to remind us that God loves us through it all.

The scriptures selected are a gentle reminder that God has chosen and loved you from the beginning—that he has a plan, a purpose, and a promise in place just for you. It is a reminder that he told us who he was in his own words. It reminds us that God's Word is active and living, and that if you meditate on and apply it, your life will simply change.

Remember just keep it simple
Love always,
—Victoria.

About the Author

Victoria Hudson is an aspiring writer with a desire to share the love of Christ via written words through fiction and nonfiction, giving believers inspiring and encouraging books that will draw them closer to God by providing reading material that teaches and reminds people of God's love and that they are not alone. She has stories to tell, and so do you. May all be blessed with gifts and talents as people glorify God.

Printed in the USA
CPSIA information can be obtained
at www.ICGtesting.com
LVHW091453141123
763892LV00051B/955

9 798888 323434